GABE: THE DOG WHO SNIFFS OUT DANGER

BY THEA FELDMAN ★ ILLUSTRATED BY CHRIS DANGER

Ready-to-Read

Simon Spotlight

New York   London   Toronto   Sydney   New Delhi

SIMON SPOTLIGHT

An imprint of Simon & Schuster Children's Publishing Division

1230 Avenue of the Americas, New York, New York 10020

© 2014 American Humane Association. The American Humane Association Hero Dog Awards™ is a trademark of American Humane Association.

All rights reserved, including the right of reproduction in whole or in part in any form.

SIMON SPOTLIGHT, READY-TO-READ, and colophon are registered trademarks of Simon & Schuster, Inc.

For information about special discounts for bulk purchases, please contact Simon & Schuster Special Sales at 1-866-506-1949 or business@simonandschuster.com.

The Simon & Schuster Speakers Bureau can bring authors to your live event. For more information or to book an event contact the Simon & Schuster Speakers Bureau at 1-866-248-3049 or visit our website at www.simonspeakers.com.

Manufactured in the United States of America 0814 LAK

First Edition

2 4 6 8 10 9 7 5 3 1

Library of Congress Cataloging-in-Publication Data

Feldman, Thea, author.

Gabe : the dog who sniffs out danger / by Thea Feldman. — First edition.

pages cm — (Ready-to-read)

"An imprint of Simon & Schuster Children's Publishing Division."

Summary: "Gabe is a real dog who works with the United States military. He has an important job: He uses his sense of smell to find weapons before they hurt anyone. Gabe saves lives! Read his story to find out more about Gabe and what makes him a hero dog." — Provided by publisher.

Audience: Ages 5–7.

ISBN 978-1-4814-2237-6 (trade paper) — ISBN 978-1-4814-2238-3 (hardcover) — ISBN 978-1-4814-2239-0 (eBook)

1. Dogs—War use—Juvenile literature. 2. Detector dogs—Juvenile literature. 3. Iraq War, 2003–2011—Juvenile literature. I. Title.

UH100.F45 2014

355.4'24—dc23

2014003906

It was a hot day in the war zone.
A group of United States soldiers
were out on a mission.
They were looking for explosives.
Gabe, a dog working in the military,
walked in front.

Gabe walked without a leash
about 100 yards ahead of
one of the soldiers.
That soldier was his partner, Chuck.
He followed Chuck's commands
for searching the steep area
by the banks of the river.

Gabe used his nose to search.
He sniffed the hot ground
and the hot, windy air.
His fur was hot.
His paws were hot too.
But Gabe did not stop.

Every step Gabe took was dangerous.
Explosives could be buried anywhere.
Some could go off if just one foot
touched the ground above them.
Gabe had four feet.
One misstep could cost him his life.

Chuck followed and watched Gabe.
All the soldiers had total faith
in Gabe.
They trusted him, and his nose,
with their lives.

Suddenly Gabe stopped.
He sat down.
This was his way of telling Chuck
he had found something.

"Come here, boy," Chuck called.
Gabe trotted over to Chuck's side.

The soldiers searched the area.
Buried under the ground
they found explosive materials
that could have been used
to hurt or kill many people.

The soldiers might not have found
the explosives without Gabe.
No person or machine can smell things
as well as a trained dog can.
Gabe saved many lives that day.
He was a hero!

The soldiers all thanked Gabe.
They rubbed his head.
They patted his side.
Chuck gave him a hug
and his favorite toy as a reward.

Back at the base, the rest of
the soldiers gathered around.
They thanked Gabe too.

The soldiers valued the work
Gabe did.
They also liked having a dog
at their base when they were so far
from home.
Everyone liked to spend time
with Gabe.

Gabe loved all the attention,
but his favorite person was Chuck.
He and Chuck were a team.
They did everything together.
They worked together and
they played together too.

Gabe had come a long way
from his days in an animal shelter
in Houston, Texas.
He did not belong to anyone then.
He did not even know how to sit
on command.

An animal rescue group stepped in. They took Gabe out of the shelter and sent him to the US Army. The army put Gabe in a program that trained dogs to find dangerous, hidden explosives.

Chuck was in the army.
He enrolled in the program
to work with dogs.
When he and Gabe met,
it was love at first sight.
Chuck liked that Gabe
was a calm and friendly dog.

The two trained together
for five months
at a military base in Texas.
Gabe learned to tune out everything
except for Chuck's voice.
Chuck learned how to understand
Gabe's smallest movements.

When Gabe and Chuck were ready,
they were sent to Iraq.

Gabe and Chuck put all their training to work. Gabe searched roadsides and riverbanks.

He searched houses and
other buildings in villages.

He searched flat, open fields,
and rocky, hilly places.

He sniffed cars that had to stop
at army checkpoints.

Some days Gabe and Chuck did not
look for explosives.
They stayed at the base
and practiced.

On other days, Gabe and Chuck
went to see wounded soldiers
in army hospitals.
Gabe wagged his tail.
He opened his mouth.
It looked like Gabe was smiling
at the patients.

Gabe cheered everyone up.
He was good medicine!

Gabe and Chuck were in Iraq
for thirteen months.
They went on more than 200 missions.
Gabe found explosives twenty-six
times.

He found more explosives than any
other dog that served in Iraq.
Gabe got forty awards
for all his hard work.
He was also named the
country's top hero dog
at the American Humane Association
Hero Dog Awards one year!

The best reward though, was that Chuck was able to adopt Gabe after Gabe retired from the army.

Gabe and Chuck visited
kids in schools.
Gabe inspired many kids.
He taught them about respect and
about doing a tough job when
it is important.

Some days Gabe just played.
He played with other dogs.
He played with Chuck.
Gabe was a hero for his country,
but he still liked to catch a ball!